Look!

Scientists believe that many years ago there was a land bridge connecting Russia to Alaska. People probably traveled across it and entered North America. What separates Russia and Alaska now?

3

The Bering Strait

ory challenge

Level 2

Level 2 history challenge

Really?

Pyramids built by Indians in South and Central America were shaped differently than those built in Egypt. How were America's pyramids different in shape from those in Egypt?

America's pyramids were stair-stepped and had flat tops; Egypt's pyramids had sloped sides and were pointed.

history challenge Level 2

Listen!

he Great Sphinx in Egypt was onstructed about 4,500 years ago. n Greek mythology the Sphinx sked passersby this riddle: What as one voice, but becomes four-ooted, is then two-footed, and then ecomes three-footed? What is the nswer?

A human—as a baby crawling on the ground, then as a person walking freely, and finally as a person using a cane

Weird!

A ring of huge stones was erected in southwestern England between 3100 and 1500 B.C. People probably used the ring for their religious ceremonies. What is the place now called?

Stonehenge

history challenge Level 2

Listen!

Herodotus, the famous Greek historian, described Persian messengers in these words: "Neither snow / nor rain / nor heat / nor gloom of night stays these couriers from the swift completion of their appointed rounds." On what federal building in New York City are these words inscribed?

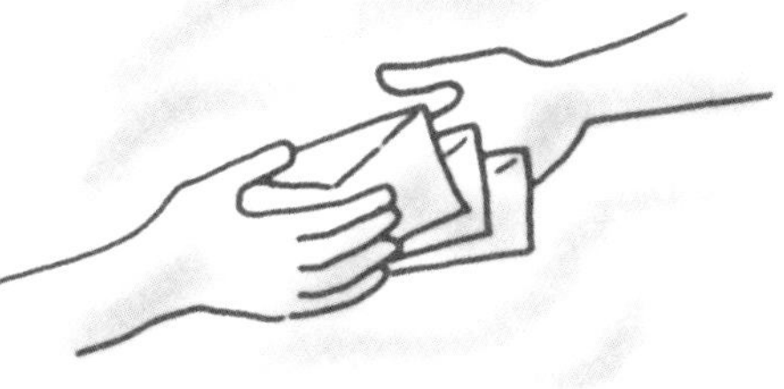

The central post office building in New York City

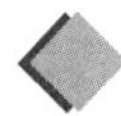      

Level 2 history challenge

Really?

The Great Wall of China, designed to stop Mongol invaders from the north, is some 4,000 miles (6,400 kilometers) long. Now that the wall is not used for defense, what purpose does it serve?

8

It is a tourist attraction.

Who Knew?

A trade route connected the ancient civilizations of Rome and China, allowing goods and ideas to travel between them. What was this route called?

The Silk Road

Writing is one of the greatest achievements in the history of the world. Around 3500 B.C., the Sumerians, invented the first writing by making wedge-shaped symbols in wet clay. What were these symbols called?

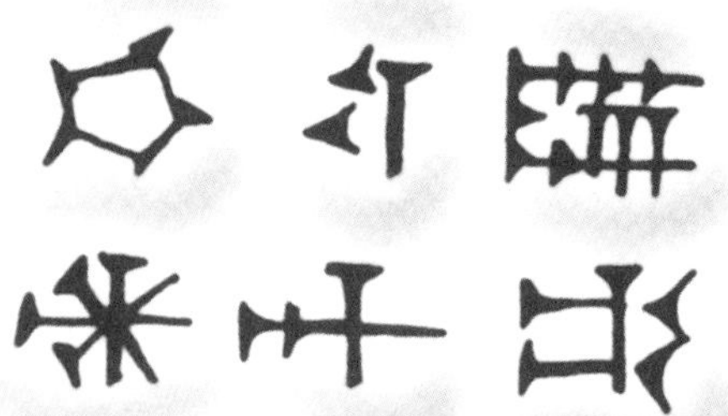

Cuneiform

history challenge

Level 2

Listen!

After a famine hit Canaan, the Israelites migrated to Egypt and lived there peacefully for many centuries until the pharaoh enslaved them in the thirteenth century B.C. Who led them back to Canaan?

Moses

 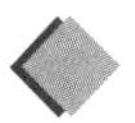     

Level 2 history challenge

Really?

In 490 B.C. an Athenian runner, Pheidippides, ran from Marathon to Athens without stopping so he could proclaim an Athenian victory over Persia. How far did he run, and what happened to him?

25 miles (40 kilometers); He fell dead after announcing the news.

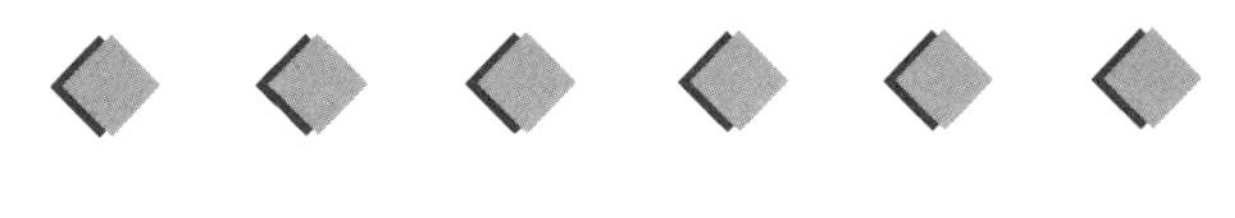

Cool!

King Nebuchadnezzar II in the sixth century, B.C., created one of the Seven Wonders of the Ancient World. What was it? Why did he supposedly build it?

The Hanging Gardens of Babylon; it is said his wife was homesick, and Nebuchadnezzar built the gardens to remind her of her home.

Level 2 history challenge

Listen!

Buddha, founder of Buddhism, lived in India around 500 B.C. He believed that by meditating, people could be released from suffering and find harmony and joy in their lives. What is this state called?

Nirvana

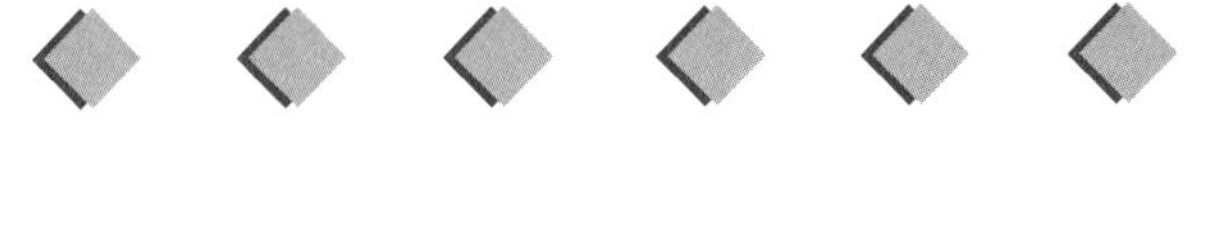

Fact!

Alexander the Great, who lived in the fourth century B.C., was 20 years old when he became king of the Macedonians and 32 years old when he died. He conquered Asia Minor, Syria, Egypt, Babylonia, and Persia. Which Greek philosopher was his tutor?

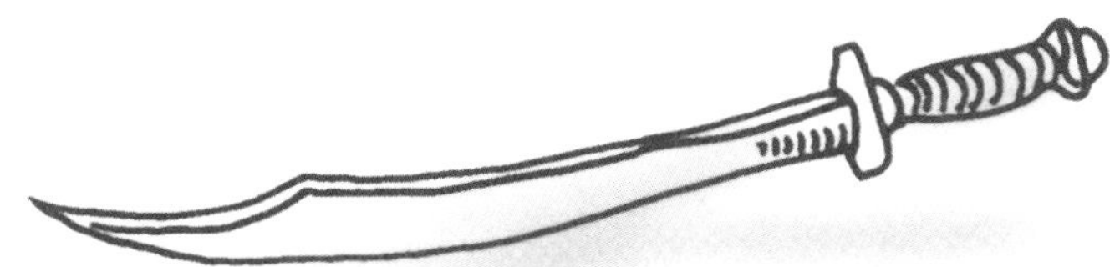

Aristotle

Who Knew?

The famous Library of Alexandria, founded by Ptolemy in the third century B.C., contained more than 400,000 scrolls. On what were they written?

Papyrus

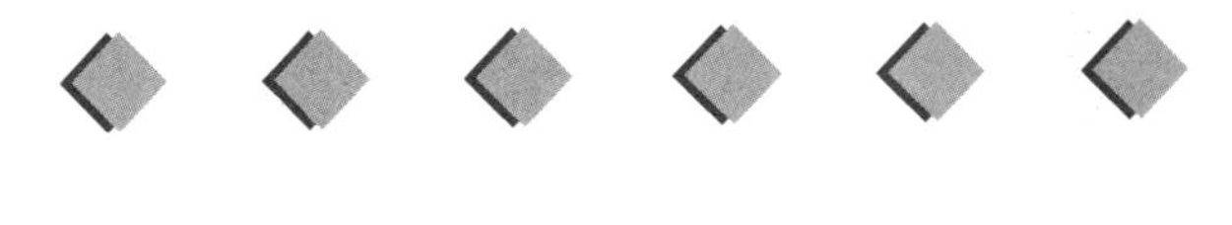

Fact!

Julius Caesar, a Roman general, came to Egypt in 48 B.C. and defeated the supporters of the young king, Ptolemy XIII, in the Egyptian civil war. Whom did Caesar place on the throne of Egypt?

He restored Ptolemy and Cleopatra as co-rulers.

Level 2 history challenge

Listen!

Confucius was a Chinese philosopher whose teachings have influenced Chinese society for two millennia. His followers put his thoughts into a book. What is its title?

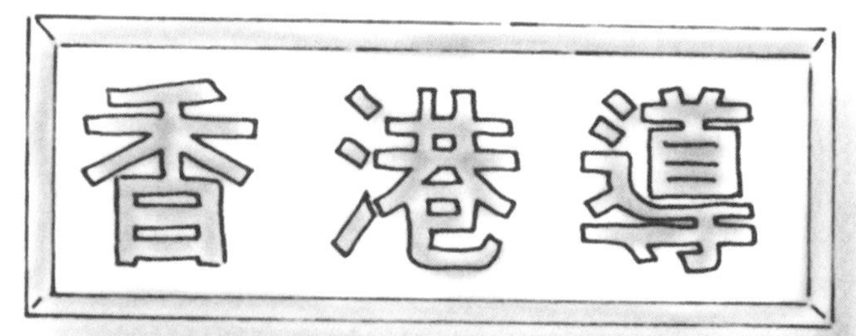

The Analects

Neat!

Hippocrates, the father of the scientific study of medicine, headed a school for physicians in Greece, where he wrote and collected many volumes on medicine. What were these called?

19

The Hippocratic corpus or Hippocratic Collection

  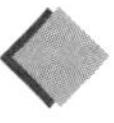     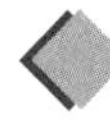

Level 2 history challenge

Really?

Galen, a famous early physician, treated the wounds of men who battled each other in coliseums. Through his work Galen discovered that blood runs through arteries. What was the profession of the men he treated?

history challenge Level 2

Fact!

Constantine was emperor of the Roman Empire in the early fourth century A.D. The capital of the empire was Constantinople. What is the city now called, and in what country is it found?

Istanbul; Turkey

Level 2 history challenge

In A.D. 529 Emperor Justinian I, head of the Byzantine (East Roman) Empire, appointed committees to update and summarize all Roman laws. What did this collection of laws become known as?

The Justinian Code

Listen!

history challenge Level 2

Islam, one of the world's largest religions, was begun by the Prophet Muhammad in the seventh century A.D. What are those who worship Islam called?

Muslims

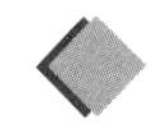

Level 2 history challenge

The Polynesians traveled long distances at sea, using wooden canoes and navigating by the stars. Between A.D. 400 and 700, they arrived in a remote island 1,200 miles away from the nearest inhabitable island. What is this island, which is famous for its giant statues?

24

Easter Island, or Rapa Nui to the original inhabitants

Who Knew?

history challenge

About the year A.D. 1002, a Norse explorer, Leif Eriksson, sailed to the coast of Canada, where he found lumber, for building ships, and grapes. What did he name the new land?

25

Vinland (Wineland)

Level 2 history challenge

The Gupta dynasty was the high point of Indian civilization. What major development do we owe to Hindu mathematicians of the fifth and sixth centuries A.D.?

They developed the decimal (base-10) number system, including the concept of zero.

Neat!

Beginning in A.D. 1173 and ending between 1360 and 1370, a bell tower was constructed on soft ground in Italy. It is eight stories high and has 300 steps that lead to the top story. What is this building called?

The Leaning Tower of Pisa

     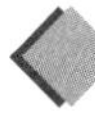 

Fact!

The Magna Carta (Great Charter) of A.D. 1215 guaranteed basic rights to people in England. What effect did the document have on the United States?

It became the framework for our Constitution.

Neat!

Indians living in the southwestern United States from about A.D. 1000 to 1300 built their homes in canyon walls under the overhangs of rocks. What were these people called?

Cliff dwellers

Level 2 history challenge

The Crusades were military expeditions in the Middle Ages led by European Christians intent on recapturing Palestine from the Muslims. Who made up the armies in two Crusades in 1212?

Children 10 to 18 years old (These are known as the Children's Crusade.)

Fact!

Feudalism was a system in the Middle Ages that protected people in western Europe when there was no strong central government. A lord gave land (a fief) to a man for his loyalty and protection. What was the man called?

Listen!

Feudalism in Japan lasted from 1192 to 1868, much longer than in Europe. What were the warlords who controlled Japan during this time called?

Shoguns

Really?

Marco Polo, an Italian traveler in the late 1200s, journeyed to China and back over the course of 24 years. What was China called in Marco Polo's time?

Cathay

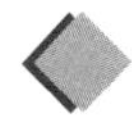      

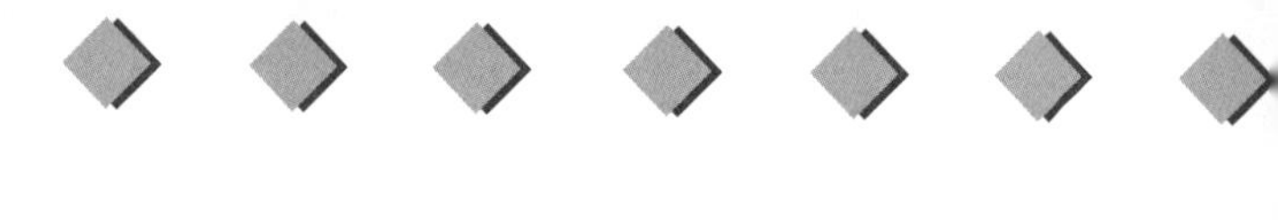

Fact!

Kublai Khan founded the Mongol dynasty in China during the 1200s and 1300s. Who was his grandfather?

34

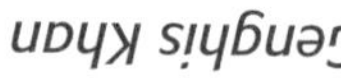

  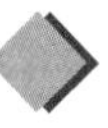     

Who Knew?

The Incas, a powerful civilization in South America from the 1100s to the 1500s, had no writing system. How do we know about their history today?

They had official "memorizers" whose job was to remember spoken stories. The Spanish conquistadors wrote down much of this oral information.

The Renaissance, a rebirth or revival of arts and literature, began in Italy in the 1300s. Renaissance Florence was ruled by the Medici family in the fifteenth century. Who was the greatest of the Medici, nicknamed "The Magnificent"?

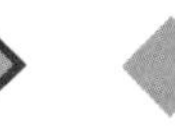

history challenge Level 2

Cool!

Michelangelo Buonarroti was an Italian sculptor, painter, architect, and poet who painted the Sistine Chapel in the Vatican. He also sculpted a famous king of Israel. Who was the king?

David

Weird!

The plague known as the Black Death killed a quarter to a third of the population of Europe in the middle 1300s. How was the disease transmitted to humans?

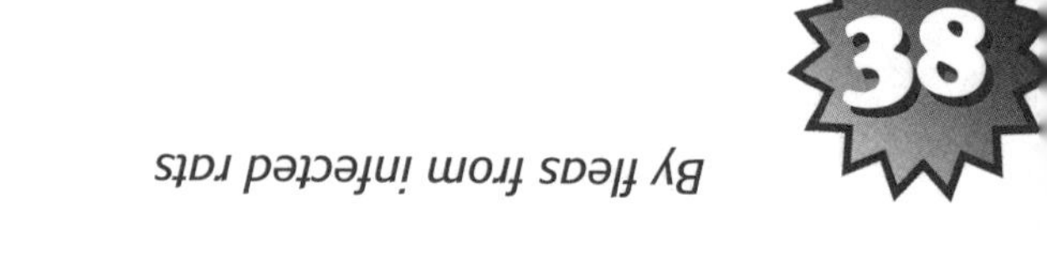

38

By fleas from infected rats

Fact!

Joan of Arc, a French military leader and heroine, led French forces to victory over the English at the city of Orléans. Later she was captured. How did she die?

She was burned at the stake.

     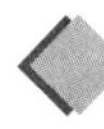 

Level 2 history challenge

The Treaty of Tordesillas in 1494 divided what is now Brazil between Spain and Portugal. What portion did Portugal receive?

40

Land east of the 46° 30' west longitude line

history challenge Level 2

Look!

The King of France sent Jacques Cartier, a French navigator, to America to find gold in 1534. What he found (in 1535) was a large river that helped France in its claim of territory. What did he name the river?

The Saint Lawrence River

Level 2 history challenge

Fact!

Henry VIII became King of England a the age of 17. He was responsible fo founding the Church of England apar from the Roman Catholic Church. How many times did Henry marry?

42

history challenge **Level 2**

Cool!

Leonardo da Vinci was an Italian artist and inventor who put many of his observations and ideas into notebooks, which contain drawings on concepts such as machines that fly, parachutes, and a movable bridge. Of his work as an artist, what are his two most famous paintings?

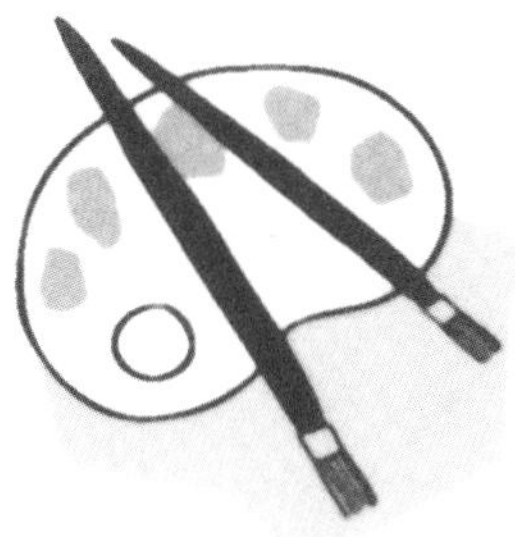

Level 2 history challenge

Listen!

John Calvin, a leader in the Protestant Reformation, enlarged upon the idea that Christianity should reform society. What were Calvin's followers called? What English group important to U.S. history did he greatly influence?

Calvinists; Puritans

history challenge Level 2

Really?

A German mapmaker, Martin Waldseemüller, suggested that an Italian-born explorer's name be used to designate the "New World" found by Christopher Columbus. What was the explorer's name?

45

Amerigo Vespucci

Level 2 history challenge

Listen!

A German monk protested certain practices of the Roman Catholic Church. This led to the Reformation, a religious movement begun in 1517, and Protestantism. What was the monk's name?

Martin Luther

Look!

A Portuguese explorer took the first European expedition around the southern tip of South America in 1520. What is the narrow waterway now called?

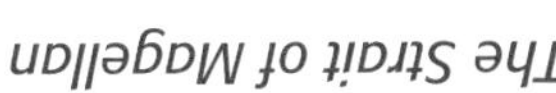

The first European expedition to explore the Mississippi River was from Spain. The explorers came in 1541 searching for gold. Who was the leader?

48

Hernando de Soto

Who Knew?

People of the Western world follow the Gregorian calendar of 1582, a calendar of 365 days in a year with a day added every fourth year. What is the year called when a day is added?

A leap year

Level 2 history challenge

Fact!

In 1588 Spain was the world's most powerful nation. Spain's "Invincible Armada" was thought to be unstoppable. What country's fleet defeated the Spanish Armada?

Neat!

William Shakespeare was an English playwright, schoolteacher, and father of three children by his wife Anne Hathaway. What was the title of his famous tragedy about two young lovers?

Romeo and Juliet

Level 2 history challenge

The capital of the province of Quebec in Canada is the city of Quebec, the oldest city (1608) in Canada. The name Quebec comes from the Algonquian Indian language and means “the river narrows here.” Who founded the city of Quebec?

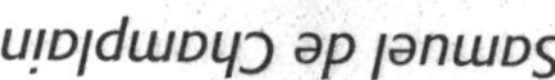

The first white explorer and his crew to see what is now the state of Delaware arrived in 1609 from England. What was the explorer's name?

Henry Hudson

Fact!

In 1670 the Hudson's Bay Company began as a group of fur traders; now it is the world's largest fur-trading company. Two French fur traders and a group of Englishmen formed the company. Who were the Frenchmen?

Médard Chouart des Groseilliers and Pierre Esprit Radisson

Really?

The first permanent English settlers in America built a colony to look for gold. When none was found, to what cash crop did the colonists turn?

Tobacco

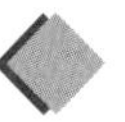

Level 2 history challenge

Look!

The British established colonies along the eastern Atlantic coast of North America and in the Caribbean. How many colonies were in America?

Fact!

Many American colonists who were loyal to Great Britain during the Revolutionary War moved to Canada, where they received free land. What were these people called?

United Empire Loyalists

 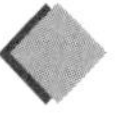     

Level 2 history challenge

The colonists in the thirteen colonies were taxed by the British without the colonists' consent. What did the colonists call this?

58

Taxation without representation

history challenge

Level 2

Listen!

René Descartes, a gifted mathematician considered the father of modern philosophy, declared in Latin, "Cogito ergo sum," which translated means, "I think, therefore I am." What does this phrase mean to you?

Responses will vary.

Level 2 history challenge

Listen!

Roger Williams believed the Indians should be paid for their land in Massachusetts, and people should have complete religious freedom. Massachusetts Bay Colony officials tried to send him back to England but he fled. What colony did he found?

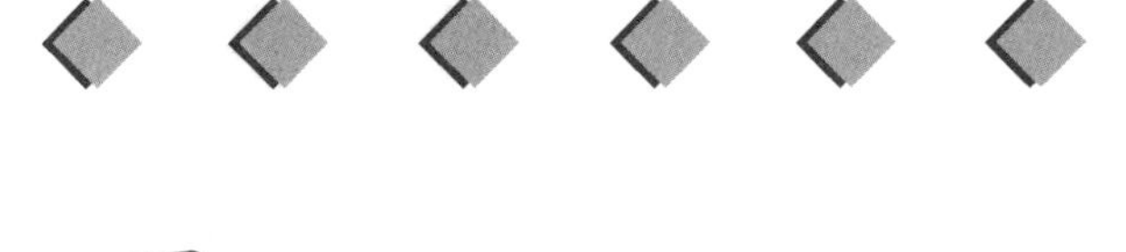

Fact!

In his early twenties, Isaac Newton made three important discoveries: the theory of gravitation; the uncovering of the secrets of lights and color; and the co-development of calculus, a kind of mathematics. What is the force that Newton discovered that keeps the earth and moon in orbit around the sun?

Gravity

  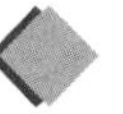    

Level 2 history challenge

The oldest institution of higher learning in the United States was founded in 1636 in Cambridge, Massachusetts. What is its name?

62

Harvard University

      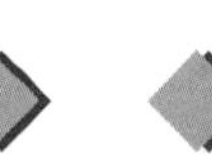

Really?

In 1788 the British First Fleet sailed into Botany Bay, Australia, with a group of about 730 European colonists. What was unique about the first colonists to settle in Australia?

They were convicted criminals deported to Australia.

Level 2 history challenge

Listen!

Peter the Great, czar and then the first emperor of Russia, made his country into a powerful nation. Peter attempted to get Russians to "Westernize." What does this mean?

64

To adopt the modern way of life of people living west of Russia

Neat!

The first public school system in colonial America was established in 1635. Later, after the colony in which it was located became a state, it was the first to require children to go to school (1852). What state is this?

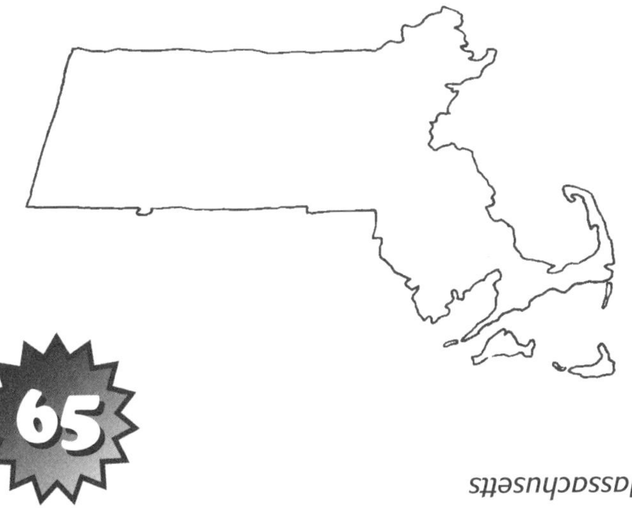

65

Massachusetts

Level 2 history challenge

In 1692 nineteen men and women were convicted of being witches and were hanged in the Salem Massachusetts Bay Colony. One hundred fifty others were put in jail. What were these trials called?

The Salem witchcraft (or witch) trials

Cool!

Freedom to print what one believes to be the truth was upheld in the American colonies in 1735. A jury found printer John Peter Zenger not guilty for printing material opposing the British governor. What amendment to the U.S. Constitution gives the press freedom to print what it considers true?

The First Amendment

Level 2 history challenge

Neat!

Sixteen-year-old Eliza Lucas Pinckney took charge of her father's plantations in South Carolina in 1739 and developed a blue dye from plants. What was the dye called?

Indigo

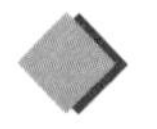      

Who Knew?

history challenge

Level 2

The *Hartford Courant* in Connecticut is the oldest continuously published newspaper in the United States. In what year did the newspaper begin publication? When did your local newspaper begin publication?

1764 (The New Hampshire Gazette, founded in 1756, also claims the title, but it joined with another paper and changed names for a time).; Responses will vary.

In 1755 the British attempted to get the Acadians, people of French origin in northeastern Canada, to take an oath of allegiance to the British king. When they wouldn't, they were forced to move south, some of them going to New Orleans. What did those who went to Louisiana become known as?

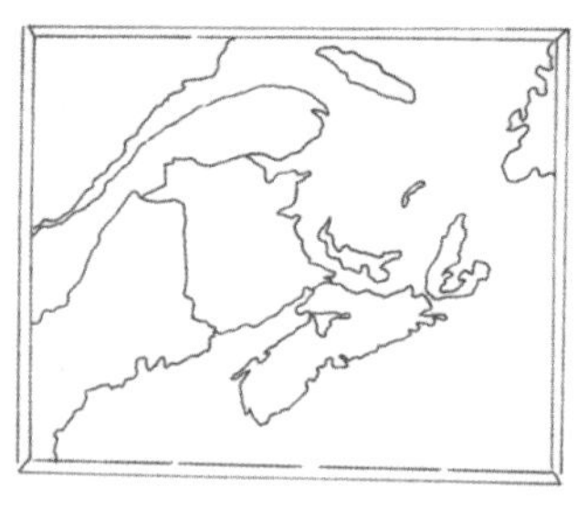

Cajuns

history challenge Level 2

Listen!

n 1776 at the age of nine, Andrew ackson read the Declaration of ndependence to his neighbors. As resident of the United States, what lid Jackson do about the national lebt that no other president has een able to do?

He paid off the last installment of the national debt.

Level 2 history challenge

Many battles were fought in New Jersey during the Revolutionary War. Because the state and its people were so important in U.S. history, New Jersey was given a nickname. What is it?

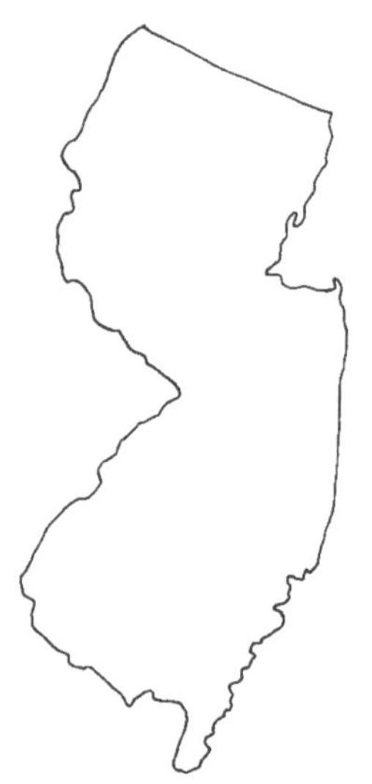

72

Cockpit of the Revolution

The French Revolution began on July 14, 1789. A prison fortress in Paris symbolized the oppressive government of King Louis XVI. Parisians captured the fortress and tore it down, and July 14 became French Independence Day. What was the prison fortress called?

The Bastille

      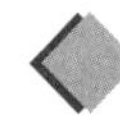

Fact!

The French Revolution was over in 1799 and the rule of French kings had ended. What general took over the government at the end of the revolution?

74

Look!

Benjamin Banneker, an African American astronomer, farmer, mathematician, and surveyor, helped lay the boundaries for an important city in the United States. What was the city?

The District of Columbia, now Washington, D.C.

75

history challenge

Level 2

In 1799, on a half-buried stone unearthed near Alexandria, Egypt, a message was found in three different languages. This stone became the key to the long-forgotten language of the ancient Egyptians. What was the name of the stone and in what languages was the message written?

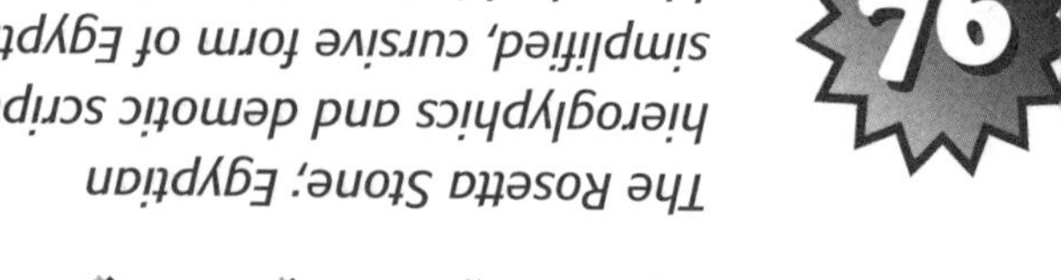

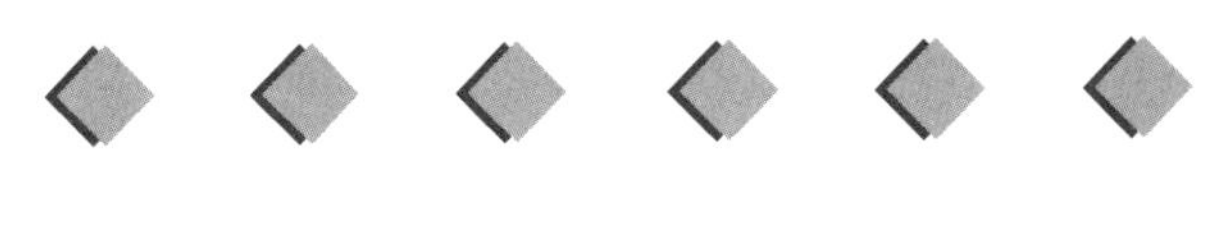

Fact!

Aaron Burr and Alexander Hamilton faced off in a duel with pistols in 1804 in Weehawken, New Jersey. Burr fatally wounded Hamilton. What high offices in government had these two men held?

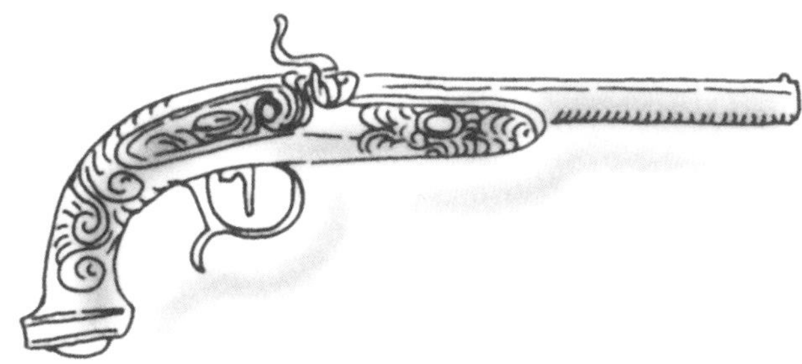

Burr was vice-president; Hamilton was secretary of the treasury

Level 2 history challenge

The Lewis and Clark Expedition traveled through the U.S. Northwest to the Pacific Ocean and back. What river did they follow to its source?

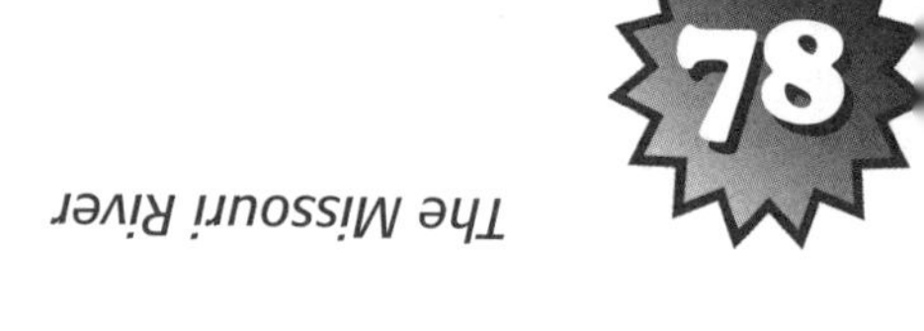

The Missouri River

history challenge

Listen!

Elbridge Gerry was the only vice-president whose name became part of the English language. As governor of the Commonwealth of Massachusetts, he signed a bill allowing voting districts to be divided to favor a specific party. What word describes this practice?

Gerrymander

Level 2

Level 2 history challenge

Really?

Jean Laffite, a smuggler, pirate, and patriot from New Orleans, led a band of seafaring outlaws. After fighting for the United States with General Andrew Jackson at the Battle of New Orleans in 1815, he received a pardon. Which U.S. president pardoned him?

80

James Madison

Fact!

President James Monroe set forth the first major policy statement of the United States in 1823—the Monroe Doctrine. What was this policy?

European countries could no longer create new colonies in North or South America.

Level 2 history challenge

The first college in the United States to accept both men and women was founded in 1833 and is located in Ohio. What is the name of the school?

Oberlin College

Fact!

The longest route for the westward expansion of the United States in the early 1800s was 2,000 miles (3,200 kilometers) long. What was the name of the route?

The Oregon Trail

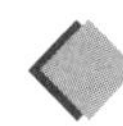  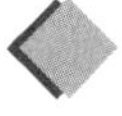    

Level 2 history challenge

Really?

Presidents of the United States must be guarded from assassination. The first attempt on a president's life was by a mentally unbalanced house painter who fired pistols at a president at close range. They fortunately misfired. Who was the president the man tried to kill?

history challenge Level 2

Fact!

A lawyer who gave up his practice in 1837 to devote his life to school reform became known as the Father of the Common Schools. What is his name?

Horace Mann

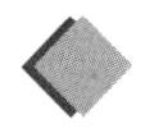      

The Aroostook War of 1839, a conflict over the border between New Brunswick, Canada, and the U.S. state of Maine, is a war that never took place. What U.S. president settled the war without military force?

86

Martin Van Buren

Neat!

history challenge

Level 2

The first women's rights convention was held in 1848 in Seneca Falls, New York. What did the women want?

87

Educational and job opportunities and the right to vote

Level 2 history challenge

Fact!

Four countries claimed some part of Oregon in the early 1800s. What were the four countries?

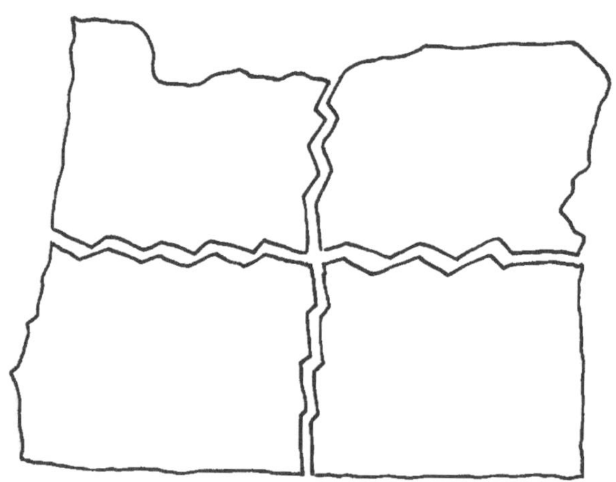

Russia, Spain, Great Britain, and the United States

Who Knew?

The first king to visit the United States was received by President Ulysses S. Grant and given a reception by Congress. Who was he, and where was he from?

David Kalakaua, King of the Sandwich Islands (Hawaii)

Florence Nightingale, a British nurse, became world-famous for her tireless efforts caring for wounded soldiers in the Crimean War. What award was she the first woman to receive?

The British Order of Merit

history challenge Level 2

Listen!

During the 1800s, boys and girls learned to read from textbooks written by American educator and clergyman William Holmes McGuffey. What were the names of these books?

The Eclectic Readers
(*Eclectic School Series*)

     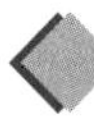 

Level 2 history challenge

Really?

Simón Bolívar, a famous South American general, won victories over Spain to win independence for Bolivia, Colombia, Ecuador, Peru, and Venezuela. What was he called by the South American people?

El Libertador (The Liberator) and the "George Washington of South America"

history challenge Level 2

Who Knew?

What is the oldest state law-enforcement agency in North America?

The Texas Rangers

Level 2 history challenge

In 1838–39 the U.S. government forced the Cherokee Indians to move from their homes in the southeastern states to Indian Territory in what is now Oklahoma. Thousands died making the trip. What was this forced march called?

94

The Trail of Tears

history challenge Level 2

Listen!

During the Mexican War of 1846–48, United States Marines entered Mexico City and raised the U.S. flag over the National Palace. The Marine Corps Hymn recounts this event in its first line. What are the words?

"From the halls of Montezuma"

 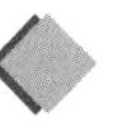     

Level 2 history challenge

Really?

Sir Richard Francis Burton, an English soldier, explorer, and speaker of forty languages and dialects, was one of the few non-Muslims to gain entrance to Mecca and live to tell about it. What body of water did he discover in 1858 in Africa?

Lake Tanganyika

   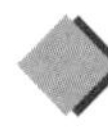   

history challenge Level 2

Fact!

A few years after the Mexican War, the United States bought a strip of land from Mexico for 10 million dollars. The land is now part of the southern ends of New Mexico and Arizona. What was the name of this agreement?

97

The Gadsden Purchase

Level 2 history challenge

Isaac Merrit Singer designed a machine that sewed stitches continuously. Because the machine was expensive, he allowed people to make small regular payments after their first payment. What did this plan of purchasing become known as? What popular household machine did Singer invent?

98

The installment plan; the sewing machine

Who Knew?

history challenge Level 2

In 1856 Margaretha Meyer Schurz began the first kindergarten in the United States. The teacher and children spoke German. In what town and state was the first kindergarten located?

Watertown, Wisconsin

Level 2 history challenge

Listen!

Dred Scott, a slave, lived for a while in areas where slavery was forbidden; therefore he sued to become a free man. The Supreme Court in 1857 denied him freedom. What happened to Scott when he was returned to his previous owner?

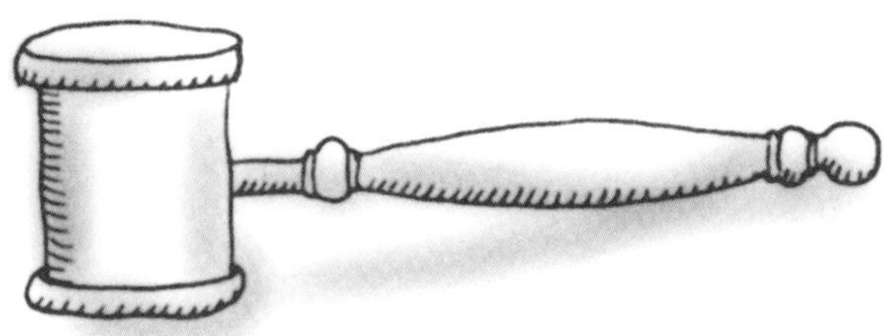

The owner (the Blow family) freed him.

Fact!

In 1859 John Brown, a radical abolitionist, attempted to free slaves by raiding the U.S. arsenal at Harpers Ferry, Virginia (now in West Virginia), to arm slaves who might rebel. Who captured him and his men?

Colonel Robert E. Lee

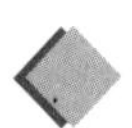      

Level 2 · history challenge

The oldest major religion on earth is Judaism. There are about 13 million Jews worldwide. What was Judaism the first religion to teach?

102

Belief in one God

Fact!

Eleven slave states seceded from the Union to form their own government after Abraham Lincoln was elected president. What did they call their new government?

The Confederate States of America

Level 2 history challenge

Listen!

The Emancipation Proclamation of January 1, 1863, ended slavery in the Confederate states fighting against the Union. What amendment to the Constitution ended slavery in every part of the United States?

104

The Thirteenth Amendment

Fact!

Appomattox Court House in Virginia was the site where the Civil War formally ended. Who were the two generals who signed the terms of the surrender?

Ulysses S. Grant for the Union, and Robert E. Lee for the Confederacy

 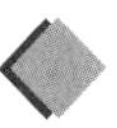     

Abraham Lincoln, sixteenth president of the United States, is considered by many to be the greatest of all the U.S. presidents.

In his Gettysburg address, what did Lincoln mean when he said, "that this nation, under God, shall have a new birth of freedom"?

Responses will vary.

  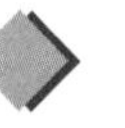    

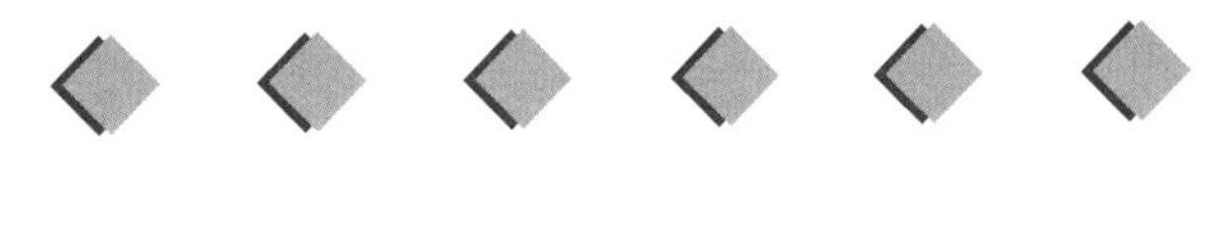

Really?

Jesse James, a train and bank robber after the Civil War, was the son of a Baptist minister. A reward of $10,000 was offered for the arrest of Jesse or his brother, Frank. Who was the gang member who killed Jesse?

Robert Ford

Level 2 history challenge

Who Knew?

During 1857–58 an American businessman, Cyrus W. Field, unsuccessfully tried to lay a transatlantic cable on the ocean floor to connect North America with Europe by telegraph. In 1866 he was successful. What countries did he connect with the line?

108

Newfoundland and Ireland

Fact!

Dynamite is an explosive with many industrial uses. Invented in 1867 by a Swedish chemist, Alfred Nobel, dynamite made possible the construction of the Panama Canal, the carvings of the U.S. presidents on Mount Rushmore, and the New York subway system. What is the oily liquid that is the explosive in dynamite?

Nitroglycerin

Level 2 history challenge

Fact!

In 1867 the Dominion of Canada was founded. Who was Canada's first prime minister?

110

Sir John A. MacDonald

Fact!

In what is now Manitoba, the settlers did not want the Red River Valley to come under Canadian government jurisdiction. This caused the Red River Rebellion of 1869 and 1870. The settlers were a mixture of white and Indian peoples. What were they called?

Métis

For 250 years Japan isolated itself from the rest of the world. In 1866, Emperor Meiji took the throne. He worked to modernize Japan, ending feudalism and isolation, and creating a parliament and a new constitution. The emperor chose the name Meiji. What does it mean?

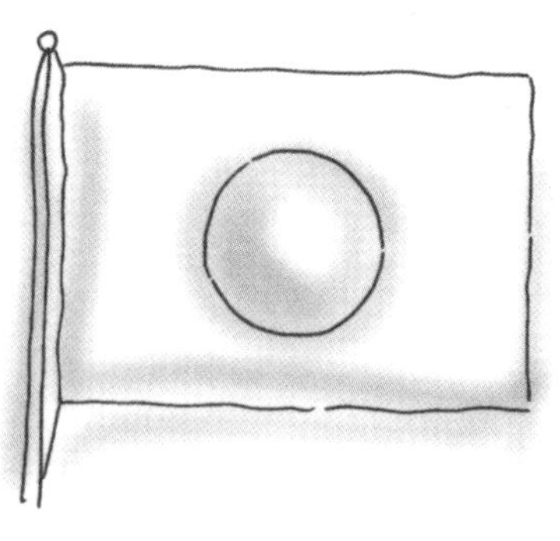

"Enlightened government"

Really?

Many U.S. citizens were disturbed because Secretary of State William H. Seward bought Alaska from Russia in 1867. They criticized him because they thought the land was only snow and ice. What did they call the purchase?

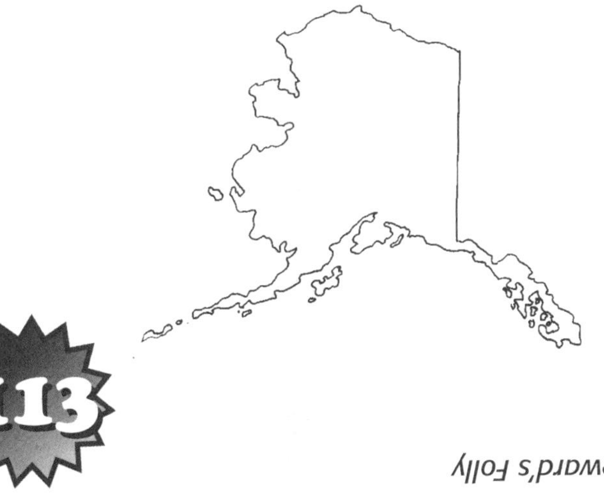

113

Seward's Folly

Level 2 history challenge

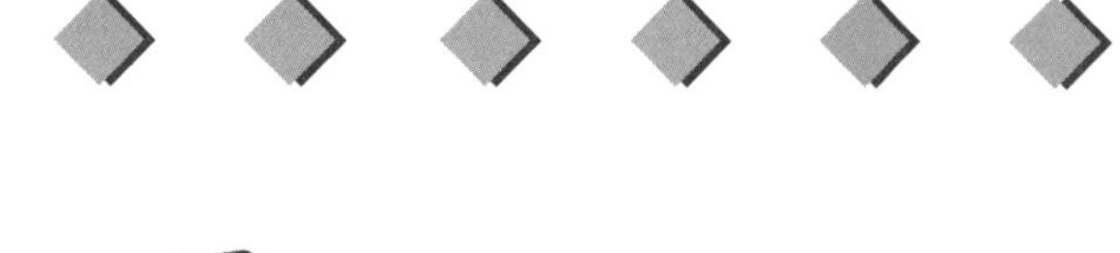

Fact!

George Armstrong Custer, a Civil War general and Indian fighter, had his last fight at the Battle of Little Bighorn on June 25, 1876. Who defeated him?

Sioux and Cheyenne warriors led by Crazy Horse and Sitting Bull

Listen!

William H. Bonney, Jr., a cattle thief and killer known as "Billy the Kid," shot two deputies to death when he escaped from jail in 1881, just before his scheduled hanging. What was the name of the sheriff who tracked him down and killed him?

Pat Garrett

Level 2 history challenge

Cool!

Alexander Graham Bell was the first to transmit human speech over a wire. He received a patent for the telephone when he was 29 years old. For what did he prefer to be remembered?

For his work as a teacher of deaf people

Fact!

Samuel Gompers left school when he was 10 years old but by 1886, when he was 36, he had organized a labor union of skilled craftsmen. He served as its president until 1924, with the exception of one year. What was the labor union?

The American Federation of Labor (AFL)

Level 2 history challenge

The Statue of Liberty is about fifteen stories high from its feet to the top of the torch. Who gave the Statue of Liberty to the people of the United States?

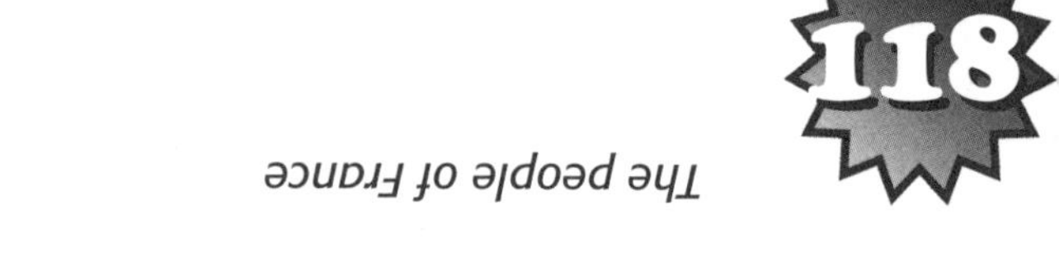

Cool!

In 1891, a physical education instructor, James Naismith, was asked by the head of his school's physical education department to create a sport that could be played indoors by several players during the winter. What was the sport he created?

Basketball

Fact!

Cyrus H. McCormick invented a horse-drawn reaping machine that could harvest 10 acres (four hectares) of grain a day. What implements did people use to harvest grain before the reaping machine?

Scythes and sickles

Really?

history challenge **Level 2**

Louis Pasteur saved many lives when he discovered that germs spread diseases. He realized that applying heat to milk killed germs and people would not get sick. What is this process called?

Pasteurization

Level 2 history challenge

Cool!

Previous to Italian Guglielmo Marconi's time, telegraph signals were sent through wire. He invented wireless telegraphy in 1895. What is another name for wireless telegraphy?

Fact!

In 1898 the U.S. battleship *Maine* went to Havana, Cuba, to protect U.S. citizens. The ship was mysteriously destroyed in an explosion, resulting in war with Spain. After defeating Spain, what land possessions did the United States receive?

Puerto Rico, Guam, and the Philippines

Level 2 history challenge

Cool!

Photographs of animals and people in motion were made by Eadweard Muybridge in the late 1800s by linking a number of cameras together and setting them off at rapid intervals as a subject passed by. What did Muybridge's project lead to?

124

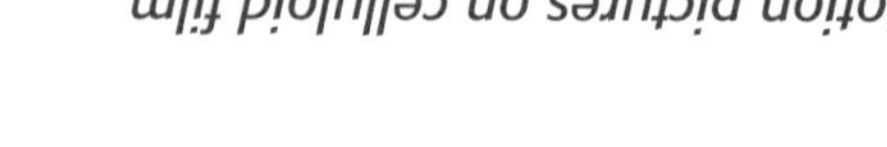

Motion pictures on celluloid film

In the 1870s Elijah McCoy, an African American engineer, invented the lubricator cup, which continuously supplied oil to various parts of many machines. What expression may have come about when people insisted on having Elijah McCoy's invention on their equipment?

The real McCoy, meaning "the real or genuine thing"

Neat!

During the 1800s, Susan B. Anthony supported causes such as abolition of slavery, the abolishment of alcoholic beverages, and the right of women to vote. She was the first woman to be pictured on a U.S. coin in general circulation. What was the coin?

A one-dollar coin

Really?

Twenty-one-year-old Frances Folsom married a 49-year-old president of the United States and became the youngest first lady in the country's history. Which president did she marry?

Grover Cleveland

Level 2 history challenge

Fact!

The Apache warrior, Geronimo, fought settlers and soldiers in Mexico and the southwestern states for many years before he surrendered. Where and how did he spend his final years?

Fort Sill, Oklahoma; as a popular attraction at fairs

Cool!

Thomas A. Edison was a brilliant inventor, industrial leader, and researcher. He worked on electrical lighting, the telegraph, the telephone, the phonograph, and motion pictures. He did all this even though he had a physical handicap. What was his handicap?

He developed hearing problems as a child.

Level 2 history challenge

Listen!

In 1896 this president was the first to use the telephone as a way of waging his political campaign. Who was he?

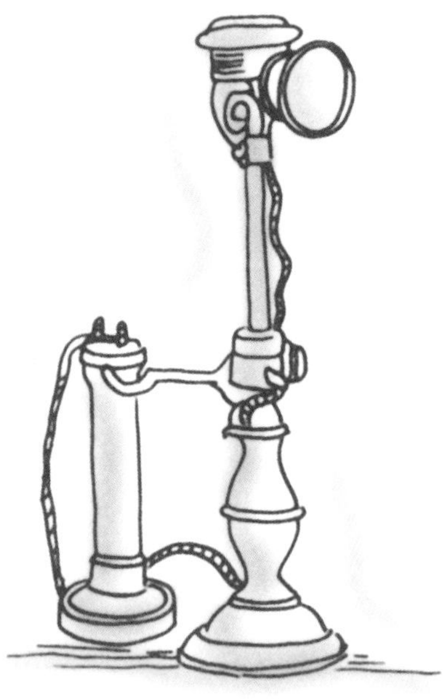

130

history challenge Level 2

Neat!

In 1903 Marie Curie became the first woman to receive the Nobel Prize (jointly with husband Pierre). In 1911 she won a second Nobel prize alone. For what did she receive the prizes?

Her work in physics and chemistry

Level 2 history challenge

Lord Baden-Powell, a British army general, began the Boy Scouts in 1907. With his sister, Agnes, he organized a similar group for girls. What was the girls' group originally called?

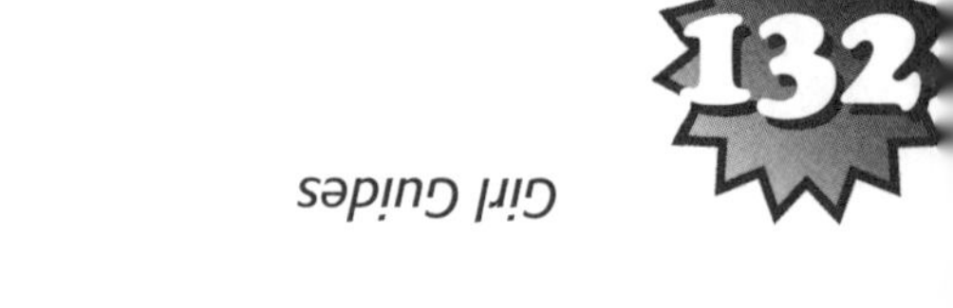

Look!

Kitty Hawk, North Carolina, was the site of the first flight of a heavier-than-air machine. Who was the pilot of this successful effort in 1903?

Orville Wright

Level 2 history challenge

Neat!

Historian and sociologist W. E. B. Du Bois, the first African American to receive a Ph.D. at Harvard, spoke out against racial discrimination. What organization did he found?

The National Association for the Advancement of Colored People (NAACP)

Fact!

Inexpensive automobiles and the gasoline to run them brought about the need for a harder rubber for tires. Charles Goodyear learned how to make rubber strong and resistant to heat and cold. What is his method called?

Vulcanization

Level 2 history challenge

Oliver Wendell Holmes, Jr., was the son of a famous writer and physician. After being seriously wounded three times during the Civil War, he studied law at Harvard. To what position did President Theodore Roosevelt appoint him?

Associate justice of the Supreme Court

Cool!

This was the first U.S. president, while in office, to ride in an automobile, ride in an airplane, receive a Nobel prize, and submerge in a submarine. Who was he?

Theodore Roosevelt

Level 2 history challenge

On February 3, 1913, an amendment to the U.S. Constitution was ratified, allowing the federal government to collect taxes on income. What amendment was this?

The Sixteenth Amendment

Really?

The first American motion-picture historical epic was a film made in 1915 about the American Civil War and its aftermath. What was it called?

139

The Birth of a Nation

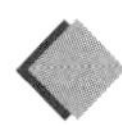   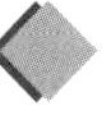   

history challenge Level 2

Who Knew?

The largest person in physical size to be president of the United States was 6 feet tall and weighed more than 300 pounds. Who was he?

William Howard Taft

Fact!

World War I (1914–18) began with the murder of Archduke Franz (or Francis) Ferdinand, who was to be the next Austrian emperor. The killing took place in Sarajevo, Austria-Hungary. What Western Hemisphere country entered the war in 1917?

The United States of America

Level 2 history challenge

Listen!

Radio became important to U.S. presidents. What president was the first to have his inauguration broadcast over the radio?

Calvin Coolidge

history challenge

Level 2

Weird!

Over the last few centuries, six different governments have ruled over what is now the state of Texas. What are the names of these governments?

United States of America, Confederate States of America, Republic of Texas, Mexico, France, and Spain

  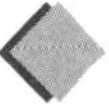    

Level 2 history challenge

State prohibition laws against drinking alcoholic beverages preceded the passage of a similar amendment to the U.S. Constitution. This amendment was the only one ever repealed. What amendment was repealed?

144

The Eighteenth Amendment

Really?

Roald Amundsen of Norway and four other men were the first to reach the South Pole. Amundsen also crossed over the North Pole. What was his means of transport over the North Pole?

A dirigible, the Norge

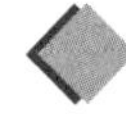

Neat!

The first person to fly alone across the Atlantic Ocean from the United States to Europe was Charles A. Lindbergh. What was the name of his plane?

The Spirit of St. Louis

Look!

In 1920 the United States granted women the right to vote. What amendment to the Constitution allowed women voting rights?

history challenge Level 2

The Nineteenth Amendment

Listen!

Sigmund Freud (1856–1939), Austrian physician and founder of psychoanalysis, believed that the mind can unconsciously repress memories going back to one's earliest days. The repressed memories can cause an illness. What did he call the illness?

Neurosis

Fact!

Kemal Atatürk, founder and first president of modern Turkey, instituted a simple Roman alphabet and insisted that every Turk have a last name. The National Assembly gave him the last name Atatürk. What does Atatürk mean?

Father of the Turks

Level 2 history challenge

Fact!

In 1929 Robert H. Goddard tested a rocket he designed. It scared people for miles around when it fell to earth and exploded. The publicity brought him funding to continue his experiments. What achievement of the space program did Goddard's experiments make possible?

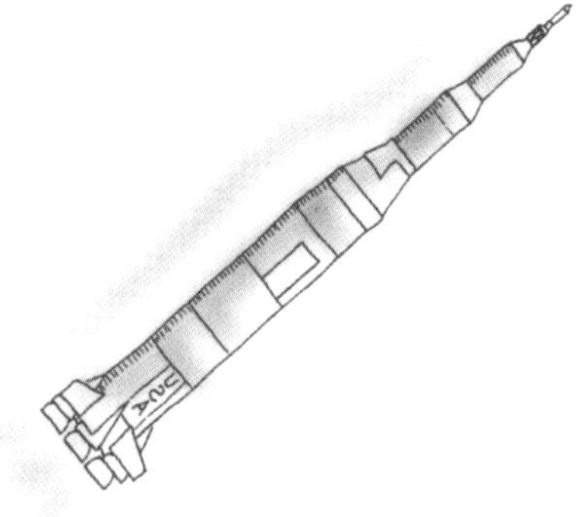

Sending men to the moon on a Saturn V rocket

Neat!

The first woman to become president of the Philippines restored democracy after the dictatorship of Ferdinand Marcos. What was her name?

Corazon Aquino

Cool!

Mary McLeod Bethune, an African American educator, was the founder of Bethune-Cookman College and worked in the administrations of four presidents of the United States. Which presidents did she serve?

Calvin Coolidge, Herbert Hoover, Franklin Roosevelt, and Harry Truman

Weird!

Alexander Fleming (1881–1955), a British bacteriologist, found some green mold destroying bacteria in a culture plate in his laboratory. What life-saving antibiotic did this discovery lead to?

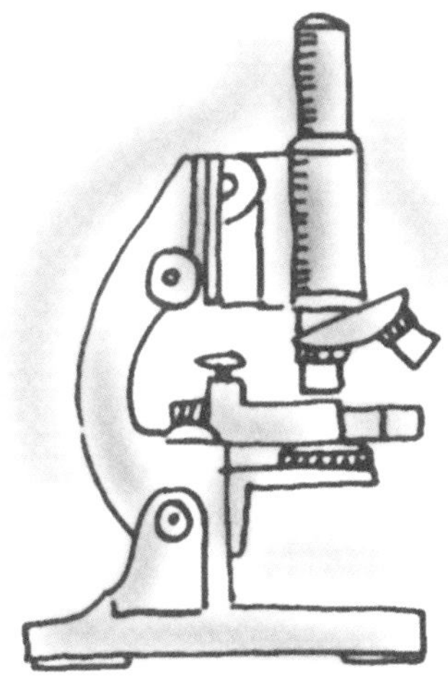

Penicillin

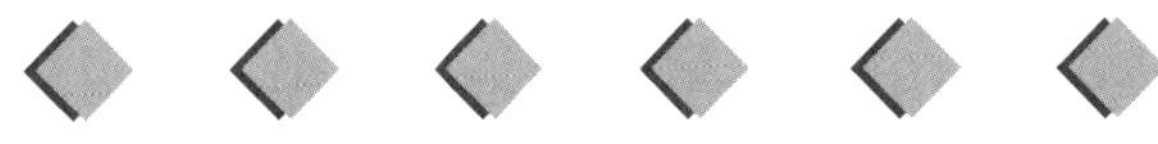

history challenge Level 2

Level 2 history challenge

Fact!

The Great Depression of the 1930s was worldwide. What do most economists think started the Great Depression?

The stock market crash on Wall Street on October 24 ("Black Thursday"), 1929

history challenge Level 2

Listen!

Novels, such as *Main Street* and *Babbitt,* helped this writer become the first American novelist to win the 1930 Nobel Prize for literature. Who was he?

Sinclair Lewis

    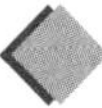  

Level 2 history challenge

Every day investors buy and sell (trade) stock on exchanges such as the New York Stock Exchange in New York City. What are the market conditions called when stock prices rise? When they fall?

156

Bull market (rise); bear market (fall)

Neat!

Nellie T. Ross was the first woman governor of a state and later was appointed director of the United States Mint. Of what state was she governor, and what president appointed her as director of the United States Mint?

Wyoming; Franklin D. Roosevelt

Level 2 history challenge

The first woman elected to both houses of the U.S. Congress was from Maine. What was her name?

Margaret Chase Smith

Fact!

Eighteen-year-olds were first allowed to vote in 1943 in this Southern state. What is the state?

Georgia

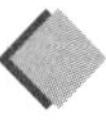

Level 2 history challenge

During World War II, the Japanese captured two islands in the Aleutian chain that are part of North America. These islands were the only land areas the Japanese were able to occupy in North America during that war. What are their names?

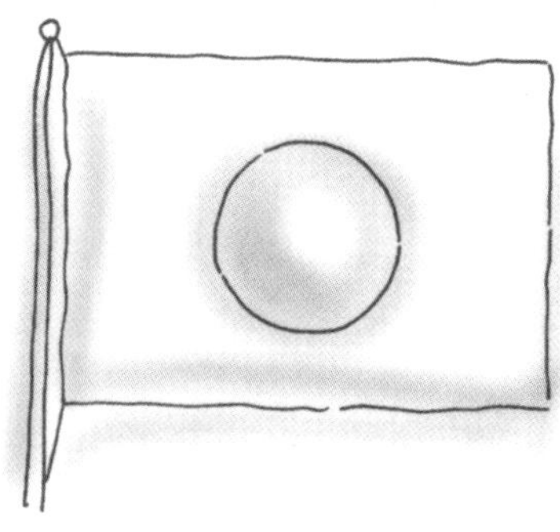

Attu and Kiska

Fact!

Japanese threats to Hawaii were ended during World War II when the U.S. Pacific Fleet defeated a much larger Japanese array of ships in June 1942. Near what island was the battle fought?

Midway Island

     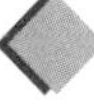  

Level 2 history challenge

Look!

One of the turning points in World War II was the Battle of Stalingrad in 1942 and 1943. This was as far as the Nazis could go into the Soviet Union. What is Stalingrad now called?

Volgograd

Fact!

Winston Churchill brought the people of the United Kingdom together against the Axis countries during World War II. What position did Churchill hold in Great Britain's government?

Prime minister

Level 2 history challenge

Listen!

Up until the early 1900s the word propaganda meant "truth." A change of meaning came when V. I. Lenin led the Russian revolution that took over Russia. What has the word come to mean now?

Responses will vary, but should contain the idea of using information to help one's cause or hinder an opposing cause.

history challenge

Neat!

The father of modern India is known to Indians as the Mahatma, or "great soul." What was his given name? What U.S. civil rights leader did he inspire with his campaign of "nonviolent noncooperation" against the British occupiers of India?

Mohandas K. Gandhi; Dr. Martin Luther King, Jr.

Level 2

Level 2 history challenge

Who Knew?

Harry S Truman had been vice-president for only 83 days when Franklin D. Roosevelt died. What was the most important decision Truman had to make?

166

Whether or not to drop the atomic bomb on Japan

Listen!

The Holocaust is a term frequently used for the German Nazi party's killing of six million Jews and other peoples during World War II. What is the word for the systematic destruction of a people because of their religion, race, or nationality?

Genocide

Oak Ridge National Laboratory in Oak Ridge, Tennessee, was build in World War II as part of the Manhattan Project. What was built there?

168

The atomic bomb

Listen!

Sir Winston Churchill, prime minister of England during World War II, used the term Iron Curtain in a speech at Westminster College in Fulton, Missouri, on March 5, 1946. The Iron Curtain separated what kinds of governments?

Democratic versus communistic

      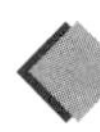

Level 2 history challenge

Rock music began in the 1950s as "rock and roll" and soon became an international music form. Who was rock music's first superstar?

170

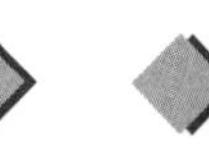

Really?

Many well-known Americans and people in government in the early 1950s were falsely accused of being communists by a U.S. senator. What was the accuser's name?

Joseph McCarthy

Neat!

During World War II, George C. Marshall commanded the largest army the United States had ever amassed and later, in 1953, won the Nobel Peace Prize. What did he do to receive the Nobel Peace Prize?

He promoted peace through the European Recovery Program (known as the Marshall Plan).

Listen!

Charles de Gaulle, a French statesman and soldier, fought against the Nazis in World War II and later led France as its president. What is the ancient Roman name for France?

Gaul

   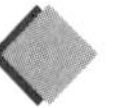   

Level 2 history challenge

Fact!

The Congress of Industrial Organizations (CIO) was a union that organized all the workers in a plant into one union. In 1955 the CIO merged with another union. What did the combined organizations become?

The American Federation of Labor and the Congress of Industrial Organizations (AFL-CIO)

Listen!

"Ask not what your country can do for you. Ask what you can do for your country." What U.S. president made this statement in his inaugural address?

John F. Kennedy

history challenge Level 2

The Soviet Union launched the first human-made satellite into space in 1957. What was it called?

Sputnik 1

  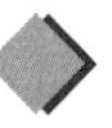    

Fact!

history challenge Level 2

In the years 1959–60, the U.S. flag gained two stars. What two states came into the United States at that time?

Alaska, forty-ninth; Hawaii, fiftieth

     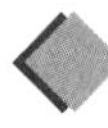 

Level 2 history challenge

The Berlin Wall, erected by the East German government in August 1961, separated the city of East Berlin from democratic West Berlin. More than 170 people died trying to escape from East Berlin, many shot by border guards. When was the wall dismantled?

November 1989

history challenge Level 2

Listen!

"I have a dream . . . that my four little children will one day live in a nation where they will not be judged by the color of their skin but by the content of their character." Who made this statement?

Dr. Martin Luther King, Jr.

Level 2 history challenge

Listen!

Biologist and science writer Rachel Carson wrote a book, *Silent Spring,* which told how some pesticides kill not only insects but birds in the same area. What are the initials of a dangerous pesticide Carson warned about in her book?

DDT (dichloro-diphenyl-trichloroethane)

Fact!

The longest war in which the United States was involved took place in Southeast Asia. What was the war?

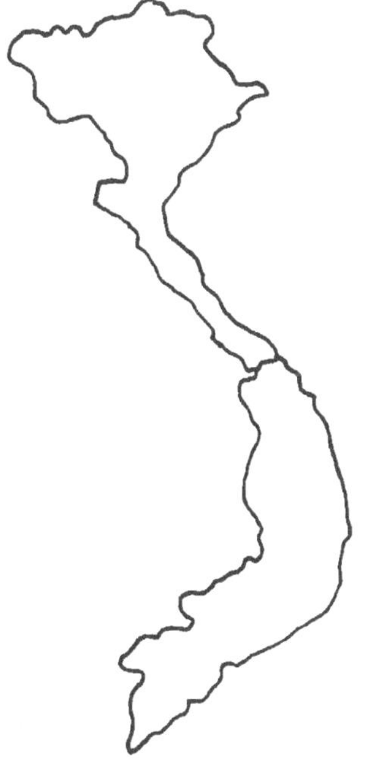

The Vietnam War (1955–75)

Really?

Ethiopia is one of the oldest countries in the world. It was also one of the first to sign the UN charter. What organization, founded in 1963, grew out of Ethiopia's efforts to end colonialism in Africa and promote cooperation among African countries?

The Organization of African Unity (since 2002, called the African Union)

Neat!

In 1967 Dr. Christiaan Barnard performed the first human heart transplant by replacing the defective heart of a 55-year-old man with that of a healthy heart from a 25-year-old woman. Where did the surgery take place?

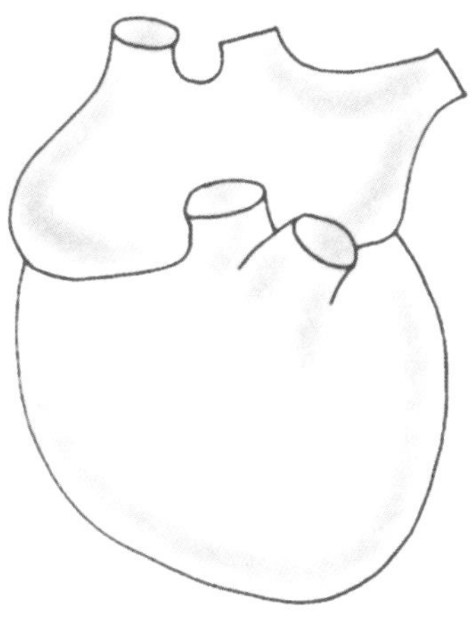

Cape Town, South Africa

  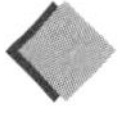     

Level 2 history challenge

Cool!

The first person to set foot on the moon was astronaut Neil Armstrong on July 20, 1969. At that time he said, “That’s one small step for a man, one giant leap for mankind.” What did he mean by that statement?

Responses will vary.

Fact!

The hydrogen bomb is much more powerful than the atomic bomb. What is the process called that combines hydrogen atoms to make helium, releasing an explosion?

Fusion

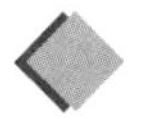

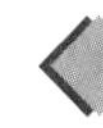

Fact!

President Richard M. Nixon resigned from office August 9, 1974, because of a scandal surrounding a break-in at the Democratic National Headquarters. What was the scandal called?

Watergate

history challenge Level 2

Neat!

Although a few women had completed their husbands' terms of office in the Senate after their spouses passed away, this woman was the first to be elected a full-term senator. Who is she, and what state is she from?

Nancy Landon Kassebaum; Kansas

 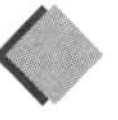 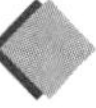    

Until 1981, the nine members of the United States Supreme Court had always been men. Who was president at that time, and what did he do to change the Supreme Court?

President Ronald Reagan appointed Sandra Day O'Connor as an associate justice.

Look!

On April 12, 1981, a space shuttle was launched by the United States. A space shuttle is a reusable manned spacecraft that can return to earth and be sent back into space again. What was the name of the first space shuttle?

Columbia

 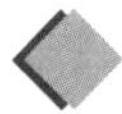     

Level 2 history challenge

Fact!

The Persian Gulf War began when Iraq invaded Kuwait in 1990. Egypt, France, Great Britain, Saudi Arabia, Syria, and the United States sided with Kuwait. What was another name for the war?

Really?

After being imprisoned for many years in South Africa, Nelson Mandela was set free. What position of leadership did he attain in South Africa?

President

Level 2 history challenge

Listen!

Under the Convention of Peking in 1860, China leased a small part of its territory to the United Kingdom. On July 1, 1997, the lease expired, and the land was returned to China, becoming a special administrative region. What is this region called?

192

Hong Kong